D0834186

GHOSTS OF THE WILD WEST

GHOSTS
of the Wild West

Enlarged Edition
Including Five Never-Before-Published Stories

NANCY ROBERTS

Photographs by Bruce Roberts

The University of South Carolina Press

© 2008 University of South Carolina

Published by the University of South Carolina Press
Columbia, South Carolina 29208

www.sc.edu/uscpress

Manufactured in the United States of America

17 16 15 14 13 12 11 10 09 08   10 9 8 7 6 5 4 3 2 1

Library of Congress Cataloging-in-Publication Data

Roberts, Nancy, 1924-
  Ghosts of the Wild West / Nancy Roberts; photographs by
    Bruce Roberts.
      v. cm.
    "Enlarged edition including five never-before-published stories."
  Contents: The last homesteaders—Deadwood, the wildest town in the
  West—The ghost and the lost treasure—The gambler of Cimarron—
  The Enchanted Mesa—Wild Bill Hickok in Abilene—The phantom
  rider of the Butterfield stage—The lovely apparition of Fort Davis—
  Pancho Villa's treasure and the ghost cat—The ghost of Cripple
  Creek—The rider wore a green habit—Indians who won't stay dead—
  The ghost light of Marfa—The sacred earth at Chimayó—The haunted
  KiMo Theater— Tombstone, Arizona, and its notorious gunfighters—
  The Enchanted Rock.
    ISBN 978-1-57003-731-3 (cloth : alk. paper)—
    ISBN 978-1-57003-732-0 (pbk. : alk. paper)
    [1. Ghosts—Fiction. 2. Short stories. 3. West (U.S.)—Fiction.]
  I. Roberts, Bruce, 1930- ill. II. Title.
    PZ7.R5442Gh 2008
    [Fic]—dc22   2007042742

This book was printed on Glatfelter Natures, a recycled paper with
50 percent postconsumer waste content.

CONTENTS

CONTENTS

PREFACE

"How did you become interested in writing ghost stories?" readers often ask. Most people want to know why an author has written a book, and they read the preface to find out. I write this for them.

It all began during a visit when my mother told me about the experience of Dr. John Allen McLean, a Presbyterian minister who was an old friend of hers. Dr. McLean was a graduate of Union Theological Seminary in Richmond, Virginia, and a very serious minded person.

While attending a party in the beautiful antebellum home of the Slocumbs in Fayetteville, North Carolina, he saw a lovely girl descending the stairs. Enthralled by her beauty, he watched her. He saw her gaze around the reception room; then she returned to the first landing. As he stood staring, she vanished. Over the years she has appeared at intervals in the house and is seen by tenants, most often on the occasion of parties. These continuing accounts, and Dr. McLean's own integrity, led me to give ghost stories more credence than ever before.

Ghosts of the Wild West came about because of my love for the West and the encouragement of the renowned Chicago author Carl Sandburg. Mr. Sandburg read my early efforts and sent a message to me at my newspaper.

"I like your stories and think they should be published in a book," he said.

Of course I agreed with his suggestion that they ought to be published in a book. At that time I was writing stories from and about the Carolinas, but the West had captured my imagination, and a few years later I began traveling out there.

I had always loved western ghost stories. They are not like the harsh stories of the convoluted Appalachians, nor do they have the romantic, magnolia redolent setting of the South. In the lawless open country of the West, the good and the bad actions of people seemed to loom larger than life. It was a perilous place with dangerous Indian tribes, precipitous mountains, treacherous canyons, life-threatening deserts—all a danger to newcomers. Survival often depended on being fast on the draw.

As I drove through the western states, I could feel the excitement that drove many to leave the East to join the gold rush. I knew that I would have gone too! There is much unusual western history in these stories. It was out west that Doc Holliday made his reputation. He left his quiet life in Georgia and became one of the most famous names of the West—although not a good role model or a man with a happy life.

The first edition of this book was a finalist for the Great Western Writers Spur Award and contains some of my favorite western characters. In revising it, I found myself reliving the lives of men and women who came

from magical places like Cimarron, Deadwood, Albuquerque, Fort Laramie, Tombstone, Cripple Creek, the
Pecos, Fort Davis, and the Enchanted Rock. I hope you
will enjoy reading about them.

And now, westward ho!

THE LAST HOMESTEADERS

They had been driving all day when the old Seth Thomas clock on the backseat began to tick. The clock was one of their prize wedding gifts, a family heirloom. The clock and the family homestead toward which they were heading, on the border of Colorado and Kansas, were two of the most unusual gifts a bride and groom ever received, as they would find out.

Joyce's mother had told her, "It's a beautiful clock, but it's somewhat like a cat for it does just what it pleases. It runs when it wants to, sometimes forward, sometimes backward." The newlyweds had smiled.

Wichita was far behind them, and in a short time they would be nearing Dodge City. Archie was driving, Joyce was sleeping, and the clock was still ticking.

Archie had taken a back road, figuring it would be a shortcut and would save him at least an hour, but the road was bleak, and in west Kansas where the rains are scarce, the land itself took on an eerie appearance toward dusk. Although the car continued to move, the land never seemed to change, always looking the same for mile after mile, almost hypnotic and as monotonous as the ticking of the clock.

It was some time after midnight when Archie noticed the highway seemed different—not really changed, just narrower. It wasn't a two-lane road any more. It was a one-lane road. Then, imperceptibly, the pavement seemed to melt into hard-packed clay, almost as if the road he knew was fading away. There was no particular point at which you could say something happened. The road simply became fainter and fainter.

Finally, about two o'clock in the morning, Archie stopped the car. He stopped because there was no road left—just the Kansas prairie stretching for miles in the moonlight. The only sound was the ticking of the clock. When the motion of the car ceased, Joyce woke up. She instinctively reached for the radio knob to turn on some music and said, "Archie, do you want me to drive for you awhile?" Archie didn't answer. Reason filtered through her senses as she awakened, and, aware that no sound came from the radio, she flipped the dial. Nothing happened, it was dead.

Then Archie's peculiar behavior caught her attention. He had gotten out of the car and was on his hands and knees in front of it, passing his hands over the ground. There seemed to be no road, and they were somewhere out on the prairie. Joyce got out of the car and looked around. Born and raised on the prairie, she was accustomed to the endless expanse of plains and sky, no towns, no farm homes lining the highway. She was unconcerned until she heard Archie repeating over and over under his breath, "It's impossible. It's just impossible! The Kansas Highway Department can't do this to me. They've built a road to nowhere. I knew our government was run by idiots, but this is incredible." Joyce sat down beside him in front of the car and said, "Archie, do you have any idea where we are?"

"No," said Archie, "but somewhere in southwest Kansas, I think. . . . I think."

He, too, had been brought up on the prairie, and knowing things always look better in the light of day, Archie suggested, "Why don't we get a blanket out of the car, snatch a few hours sleep, and in the morning we'll go back and find that highway." The stars were bright. There was a faint sweet fragrance in the air, and the pair soon drifted off to sleep. The only sound was the tick of the clock coming from the backseat of the car.

The sun was well up in the eastern sky when Joyce opened her eyes, stretched, and saw a covered wagon and oxen standing a few feet away. How quaint, she thought. I wonder where that came from. Archie was still sleeping as she walked over to it. It was just like those she had seen in all the old pictures, but somehow she seemed to feel a special affinity for this particular wagon. The oxen were yoked and appeared to be contentedly waiting for someone to climb aboard. She and

Archie had had an old-fashioned wedding, and everyone had worn period clothes. Now she looked down at her dress and realized that it was really just perfect with the wagon—like something out of a book.

At that point she realized their car was missing. There was no car anywhere, in fact the wagon was where the car should have been. As she stood beside the wagon, she heard the ticking of a clock. She peered in, and there it was—the old Seth Thomas clock. It was now running forward instead of backward!

Joyce looked beyond the wagon, and less than half a mile away was the family homestead looking just as it had in the framed photograph on the dining room wall of her parents' house in Wichita.

As she walked behind the wagon, she noticed a very interesting thing. Leading up to the rear wheels were the marks of automobile tires. They stopped a few inches from the wagon wheel. She went over and hugged Archie until he woke up.

"We have gotten the most unusual wedding present anyone ever got. Just wait until you see it."

"Really, did they deliver it out here in the middle of the prairie?" said Archie sleepily.

"Archie, what was out here in, say, about the 1860s?"

"Oh, Apaches, buffalo, all that sort of thing. Not too much really, but what were you saying about a wedding present?"

"I was going to say the present is that we're going back to the land, back to the first homestead."

"Of course, I know that."

4

"But, Archie, it's all real. My mother was right about that clock; it took us straight back in time. How would you like to find that we're our own grandparents!"

DEADWOOD, THE WILDEST TOWN IN THE WEST

It was August of 1876 and Seth Bullock, sheriff of Montana's Lewis and Clark County, was becoming restless. He and his friend Sol Star were partners in a hardware store, but it held little promise.

"The place where the market for this stuff is really booming is the gold country," said Seth enthusiastically. "I hear folks are buying pots and pans and hammers and nails out there hand over fist."

"You mean places like Deadwood, South Dakota?" said Sol.

"That's right."

"Haven't you heard the reputation of that town? It's famous for being the rowdiest, most lawless place in the West!"

"And Deadwood is just where I would like to go."

He was not to be discouraged, and a few weeks later he and a reluctant Sol set out for South Dakota with three wagonloads of merchandise. Dust rose above their wagons. When they reached Deadwood, it was a warm day and the sky hung over them like the interior of a round blue bowl.

In the rooming house where they would be staying, Seth opened the small black trunk that held his personal possessions. He and Sol would be living in this boardinghouse for a while and eating their meals side by side with the other new arrivals. He withdrew the leather Bible his mother had given him and placed it on the bedside table next to the kerosene lamp. His father, George Bullock, had been a retired major in the British army and, some said, almost too strict a man. Both parents had instilled a strong faith and a sense of duty in Seth.

An hour later he and Sol began putting up a tent, which would be their temporary store. There was much interest in their preparations, and they were soon surrounded by a crowd of curious men. There were almost no women in the gold-rush towns of those days.

Their wagons held everything the settlers and gold prospectors arriving in Deadwood almost daily needed to set up housekeeping. Pots and pans, kettles and boilers, chamber pots and washbowls sold as fast as Sol and Seth could unpack them from their wrappings.

But as Sol had predicted, peace and quiet did not last long. On the afternoon of August 2, 1876, their second day in Deadwood, shots rang out. Seth forgot everything else. All the reactions of a lawman surged up within him. Noting the direction the sound of the gun came from, Seth began racing down the street toward Nuttall and Mann's saloon.

He burst through the swinging doors to find the notorious Wild Bill Hickok, whom he had met only the night before, fallen back in his chair. There was a hushed silence in the saloon. A few minutes ago Wild Bill had been sitting quietly playing cards. Seth ran over to him, but Wild Bill was beyond help. Blood poured from a gaping wound at the back of his head. He had died instantly.

It was not long before the men sitting at the bar recovered from the shock and pandemonium broke loose. Everyone knew Hickok. Colorful, reckless, he would become one of the legendary characters of the West.

The saloon and soon the people of Deadwood were in an uproar over his unprovoked murder. McCall was strutting all over town bragging, "I killed Wild Bill, and I don't mind telling everybody. He killed my brother!"

"What brother?" someone shouted.

McCall's voice was shrill as he answered. "My brother back in Abilene, Kansas, that's who. Why Hickok shot him down like a dog. I'm glad I shot him. Wild Bill deserved to die."

But it was soon discovered that McCall never had a brother. Sitting at the bar, growing more drunk by the minute, he had simply turned around, seen Hickok, walked over and shot him in cold blood.

To the town's shock, an impromptu court declared McCall not guilty! Seth Bullock did not hesitate to express his outrage, and his manner elicited respect.

Justice was to come later. McCall's trial was declared to have no legal basis in the Indian Territory of Deadwood. But we are getting ahead of our story.

Only a few days had passed when Seth was walking down the street and met a tall imposing fellow. Seth knew immediately who this man was, and after greeting him courteously, he came right to the point.

"Your services are not needed here, so I suggest you be on your way." The man he was speaking to was Wyatt Earp, the famous marshal of Dodge City, who was probably in Deadwood prospecting for the sheriff's job. Earp left town a week later to return to Dodge.

Bullock seemed to know even then that the job of sheriff of Deadwood was cut out for him. It was not long before admiration for this former lawman from Montana, and an increasing outcry for law and order in the town, earned Seth Bullock the position of sheriff of Deadwood. Now it would be up to him to clean up the wildest town in the West.

Amazingly enough, he did it without ever killing anyone! He was a man who had an unbendable sense of morality and duty, and it impressed those who met him. They say Bullock's reputation for being completely fearless was such that shady characters could not meet his stern, unwavering gaze.

Bullock and Star's hardware store burned in 1894, and what could have been disaster became opportunity. On the same site Bullock built Deadwood's first hotel—a sixty-four-room luxury hotel. Bullock himself lived there. He was a man of fine character and great strength of personality. The one-time Deadwood sheriff went on to become a United States marshal, an outstanding conservationist, and a good friend of Teddy Roosevelt's.

Proud of the reputation of the hotel named after him and of the kind of guests that stayed here, he made sure it stayed that way. He was living there in room 211 at the time he died of cancer in 1919.

Famous people, wealthy people arrived through the years to enjoy the comfort and the scenic attractions of this historic gold-rush town. But not all visitors were equally desirable. The gentleman we are about to mention falls into this category.

Wally Warfield had planned his visit to Deadwood carefully. He was a hit man. His victim was to arrive at the Bullock Hotel the same day he was and had reserved a room on the third floor. The man he was to meet, Magiani, was a serious risk to the mob. Warfield had reserved the room next to his. The night of his arrival, Wally left his luggage in his room, without bothering to unpack, and went down to gamble in the casino.

Some hours later, after several hands of poker, Warfield started up to his room. He couldn't find it at first, but he met a tall, courteous man who helped him.

"You are in room 311? Here we go. Up the steps. Careful there. Here is your hall. Let me open the door to your room for you." The man reached down, pulled a key from his own pocket, and opened the door to the room. There was Wally's luggage inside, just as he had left it.

Well, he would rest for a couple of hours before he visited room 313 next door. Give the fellow a few minutes to sleep before he sent him into that deep sleep from which there is no earthly awakening. Wally lay down for a minute on the bed, and before he knew it, he was out—possibly a combination of fatigue and too much Jack Daniel's whiskey. He did not awaken until almost eight the next morning!

Opening his briefcase, he quickly strapped on his small gun with the silencer and went out into the hall. Walking a few steps to the room next to his, he looked up at the door and was startled to see that it was not 313 but 213! He had made his reservations at the Bullock Hotel and been promised the third floor. What else could go wrong here? Now he was furious. He would check on Magiani.

He went down to talk with the desk clerk.

"Your man put me in the wrong room last night."

"What room did he place you in?

"Room 211. I was supposed to be in 311."

"Was your luggage in it, sir?"

"Of course, it was or I would have notified the desk immediately!

Now—would you please ring me room 313."

"The one next to yours?" The manager began looking at the guest list. "Of course. That would be Mr. Magiani from Chicago. Oh, I'm sorry, sir. He checked out at six o'clock this morning."

Wally Warfield cursed inwardly. "I would like to get hold of that employee of yours who put me in the wrong room!"

"That room is closed. You say one of our staff put you in 211? Who?"

"How should I know! He was tall and slender with a wide bushy mustache and the most piercing eyes I ever saw."

"We have no one here who looks like that—at least no one living now, sir."

"What do you mean *no one living now*?

The desk clerk replied, "Years ago this hotel was owned by a man who met that description. He was Sheriff Seth Bullock. People say that he was as fine a man as you'll ever meet. And that even today his ghost comes back to protect the hotel and guests from any harm. Just a story of course. Here's a picture of him, sir." It was the man with the piercing eyes.

Warfield's face whitened. "Rot!" he exploded angrily.

"No offense meant, sir," said the desk clerk. "But you'll be interested to know he died of cancer in that very room you say you stayed in. He's one of those legends of the Old West. I think I can find some stories on him right in one of these drawers. Would you like to know more about him?"

But when he looked up, his guest was gone.

The Bullock Hotel operates to this day and now has a twenty-four-hour casino. Deadwood is one of the most fascinating and well-preserved towns of the West. The entire town of Deadwood has been designated as a historic site.

THE GHOST AND
THE LOST TREASURE

The West abounds with spine-chilling stories of ghosts and lost mines. Somewhere in a stream in Colorado is a wooden chest full of gold coins, and a ghost there may go on forever trying to reveal the location of the treasure. There are those who claim to have seen him, but will anyone ever hear him?

Fort Garland, which was commanded by Kit Carson, is in the San Luis Valley of southern Colorado. Built of adobe and massive pine beams, the buildings were across the ancestral trail of the Indians. Danger was always near and there was little to amuse the men at this lonely outpost, but the paymaster was an experienced fisherman, and he had several friends who took pleasure in joining him. They were older men who were not afraid of the haunted, snow-covered ridges to the south or the secret canyons through which the Trinchera flowed.

One day in late spring the paymaster left the fort in a horse-drawn wagon with a guard of four mounted soldiers. He was heading south to Fort Union, New Mexico, to bring back the payroll for the men and officers of Fort Garland.

The paymaster didn't worry about the trip back. He knew the country well, and he was a brave man. Finally he was only a few miles from the fort. It was late afternoon, and as he rode through some of his favorite fishing country, he thought he would soon be back this way with some of his friends. The horses clattered down the steep, winding grade along Trinchera Creek.

Just as they reached a flat area opposite the entrance to Gray Back Gulch, the sharp ra-ta-ta-tat of gunshots broke the quiet mountain air. The four guards dropped from their horses, riddled by bullets. The horses pulling the wagon spooked and began to race down the twisting, narrow road, the bandits in pursuit. The paymaster was mortally wounded, but he still was not dead. He managed to pull the iron-bound box up onto his knees and struggled to keep his balance in the wildly lurching wagon as he waited for the right place in the road. Soon the road would sweep in close to Trinchera Creek and to the deep hole where he had often fished.

There it was! With one last effort the dying man heaved the heavy paychest from the wagon, and it landed with a loud splash right in the center of the deepest water. The paymaster fell back unconscious,

and the panicked horses dashed on. A few minutes later the lookout at the fort saw the wagon coming at a wild pace surrounded by a cloud of dust. He was astonished to see that it was driverless, and he began to shout. Men began pouring out of the fort to watch the approach of the wagon.

Mounted soldiers raced along to catch up with it and managed to stop the lathered horses. They found the paymaster lying in the wagon half-conscious. "The chest," said the paymaster weakly, "it's in my favorite fishing hole. Ask . . . ask my friends . . . it's near—" And with that the brave man died.

Men leaped quickly on their horses to chase the fleeing bandits, and others were dispatched to bring in the bodies of the four guards. All were dead, and they were brought back to be buried on the windswept hill north of Fort Garland. Another detachment was sent to search the waters of Trinchera Creek, and they began at the place where the first men fell. But they found nothing. One friend after another felt sure he could find the favorite fishing hole, but each time there was nothing on the bottom of the creek but rocks.

It was only a few weeks later that the ghost was first seen by two troopers on duty. Thinking it was some dreadfully wounded officer who had made his escape from an Indian ambush, they shouted for the sergeant of the guard and, with a few startled troopers, dashed from the gates to assist the wounded man. But even as they ran toward him, the figure dissolved like a cloud in the sky, the blue fading into the gray of the sagebrush. Imploring eyes seemed to plead for help until the very last, and then there was nothing—only the echo of the wind through the valley and the reddish glow of the sun on the looming Sangre de Cristo Mountains in the dusk.

Years later when the fort was restored, the old wooden building, once the headquarters, was made a museum. The people who used this room have been re-created in wax, and so cleverly done are they that they might pass for real people. At the desk sits Commandant Kit Carson, the blue uniform covering his waxen shoulders.

It is here that the ghost has been seen late at night wearing a blood-stained blue uniform and standing near the commandant's desk as if he is trying to tell him something. He lifts his arm to point, and then, as if sensing that ghosts are sometimes blocked from communication with human beings and even with the waxen figures of former comrades who are now, also, dead, the shadowy specter disappears as mysteriously as it comes.

Once a real man, the ghost still haunts the fort entreating someone to listen. And today, somewhere at the bottom of a deep pool in Trinchera Creek is a chest full of gold.

THE GAMBLER OF CIMARRON

"Last year we went to an island in the Caribbean. What would you think about our going on a trip out to the Southwest?" Roger asked.

"Mmmm. Sounds interesting," Joan murmured with mild enthusiasm. "But nothing phony."

Roger was encouraged. He was worried about his wife's depression. For the first time since her father's death, Joan's voice held some interest in something.

"What do you mean nothing phony?" her husband said.

"I just meant not a theme park sort of thing. I would like for it to feel authentic—as if I have been transported to what the Old West was really like."

"That's a big order. No, this isn't a resort, honey. It's a town—a real town named Cimarron."

"I've heard of the book by Edna Ferber. Later it was made into a movie, wasn't it? And this is the place?"

"No. This is in northeastern New Mexico—beautiful country—and I think you are going to like it."

She had been agreeable on the trip, but her depression had seemed to return. She was far from her vibrant self even when he pointed out the beauty of the Sangre de Cristo Mountains. It was late afternoon, and Joan napped the last few miles. When she awoke, it was to see an enormous elk just outside the window on her side of the car. "Heavens!" she cried out, throwing up her hands in amazement. The animal drew back, avoiding their Land Rover, but was so close its brown coat almost brushed the car.

Even in the heart of town the presence of elk, buffalo, and antelope did not seem to be unusual. This was the way the surrounding grasslands had probably looked a century or two ago. They were in the broad valley of the Cimarron River, and before them was their destination

The St. James Hotel was a long two-story stucco building, golden in the sunlight like many of the early western buildings. Joan stepped into its lobby and looked up into the faces of mounted deer and buffalo staring down at her from the walls. For a moment she began to feel really part of this scene. Wasn't this what it would be like to live in the Old West—the Victorian furniture, velvet drapes, antique chandeliers, and brocade wallpaper?

What was the desk clerk asking her husband?

"Do you want to be in the one of the fourteen rooms of the main hotel with no phone, no radio, and no television, or would you prefer the ten-room annex and all the conveniences of a more modern hotel?"

She didn't know what possessed her, but she spoke up and said, "I would like to stay in the main part of the hotel without a TV or telephone in our room to bother us."

"Yes, ma'am," said the clerk, but her husband protested. "Joan, are you sure this is what you really want? Your know we are used to just picking up the phone and calling some friend on the other side of the world."

"Who do we need to call? I talked with Mother and Dad this afternoon, and they said everything was fine. They know that we will be at the hotel here."

"Fine. Then let's go down to the dining room."

After dinner they took a walk and about nine o'clock returned to the hotel. Joan had bought a book about Cimarron and wanted to read in the room.

"Hello, cowboy," a voice called from the dining room as they passed, and looking in, Roger saw two men at a table, playing cards.

"How about joining us?" said a middle-aged man whose western hat was tilted rakishly back on his head.

Roger paused and looked in. "Do you mind, honey?" he asked and turned back to his wife.

"Just so it's for fun and not money," Joan said with an anxious look at him.

There was a flash of anger in his eyes. "And why not?"

"Because the last time you did that you lost half of the money we were going to pay Dad for a share in his business. I think that horrible man becoming part owner instead of us played a part in his heart attack."

"Look at the money I won later that paid for the Caribbean trip last year."

"I wish the winnings amounted to half of what you have lost, Roger."

"Oh, don't start that again. I don't want to hear it!"

"Roger, that doesn't sound like you! You promised me you would stop."

"I'm sorry, Joan, I know I did. And I'm not doing any serious gambling. You know that. I won't be long."

"Deal me in," said Roger as he pulled up a chair, and the hands of the man with the western hat and the steel-gray eyes moved so quickly that within seconds Roger's cards were on the table before him. Two hours flew by, and the room filled with smoke that stung Roger's eyes. His hands were unusually good, and he had a drink or two to celebrate.

The man in the western hat leaned back in his chair, his eyes no longer friendly.

"That's it! Tryin' to make me think you're just a tenderfoot at this game, aren't you, boy!" And he pushed the winnings toward Roger. Clapping his hat on, he rose to go. "I'm turning in, boys," he said and started toward his room.

Roger walked after him a little unsteadily. The hall seemed filled with a gray mist. How could smoke be out here? he wondered. But he managed to keep the man in sight until he saw him entering a room some distance ahead. He was almost there when he felt a sudden piercing pain between his shoulders and realized it felt the way a bullet must feel. He stumbled but went on. Somehow he must reach that door.

Then he saw a horrifying face. It was the face of the man he had played poker with hanging in the middle of a flaming red cloud!

Then it began to speak. "You're coming, aren't you? I saw you when you registered today, and when I first looked at you, I knew you were mine. I'm ready to take you with me tonight." Roger felt himself losing consciousness as he fell against the door of room 18.

Joan woke up in the middle of the night to a loud knock.

"Ma'am, I think we need to see about your husband."

"See about him? Isn't he all right?"

"No. He's not. He is lying on the floor in front of the door to room 18. I heard him groan and call out, 'I've been shot,' and then, 'God help me!' So I went running."

"I thought he was playing poker with some other men."

"He sat at a table, but when the evening ended there was only one man playing cards with him. A stranger whom I have never seen in this hotel before. Then, begging your pardon, ma'am, but your husband had several drinks, and he seemed to be upset. When I next saw him, he was in the hall, lying on the floor groaning."

"You will need someone to help you bring him to our room," Joan said. "Shouldn't we knock on this door?"

"No, ma'am. Not that door. That's room 18. It's the haunted one." *He's crazy,* she thought. At that moment the night manager came by, and to Joan's relief they half dragged, half carried Roger to their room.

All night he tossed and turned, and for a man uninterested in religion, his wife heard him mention God several times. He winced when he turned over and told her his back hurt because he had been shot. She found a dark bruise on his back but no trace of a bleeding wound.

"It was dreadful to find you out there in the hall lying on the floor. Do you know where you were, Roger?" He shook his head. Joan continued, "Have you heard the story that room 18 is haunted by a gambler named T. D. Wright? He is a man that an angry loser killed after the game. He had won everything from the other gambler—I guess it was like the night you gambled away all the money you had saved to buy a share of Dad's business."

"I don't want to hear about that!" Roger burst out.

"Just let me tell you about Mr. Wright. It's quite a story. The man who had lost everything followed him and shot him in the back just as Wright reached his room—where you were found outside the door—he bled to death inside. They say Wright was known as an ill-tempered man."

Roger felt for his wallet and looked in it nervously to see if he could reconstruct the events of the night before. Beginning to count his money, to his amazement, he counted out far more than he had brought with him! He had won considerably more than he had realized.

His wife patted him on the back. "I'm so glad you stuck to your promise to me and didn't lose any money, dear."

Roger winced at another pain in his back, and an expression of horror began to cross his face. He dimly recalled seeing something or someone in front of the door to room 18, the room in which Wright was shot. Was that some strange sort of warning to him? Perhaps his destiny? Had he narrowly escaped death? The terrible bruise on his back hurt whenever he moved. In any case he found that he had lost all interest in gambling —perhaps for the rest of his life.

Room 18 has been left much as it was in the days of the Old West. It is considered by the staff of the hotel to be haunted, and guests are rarely allowed to enter. But if you would like to investigate it, someone on the staff might oblige.

There are fascinating history tours to take in Cimarron, New Mexico. Let the U.S. Park Service guide you around.

THE ENCHANTED MESA

For many years the two professors shared an interest in the supernatural. Now Cardoza stole a glance at Montana, who was driving, and for the first time he became uneasy. There was a fanatic look about his face, and all of Dr. Cardoza's efforts to joke about why they were driving out here in the middle of the night were meeting with no response.

Joseph Montana drove on through the barren country among towering, grotesque mountain formations that appeared eerie indeed in the light of the full moon. This was the road to the Enchanted Mesa, southwest of Albuquerque. Montana had written asking him to leave his work in Tucson, fly to Albuquerque, and drive out here with him tonight. They had come here many times as boys, and he knew the tragic story of the mesa had held a strong fascination for Montana even when they were young, but that was years ago. What could he possibly be up to tonight? They drove in silence, as Montana did not seem inclined to talk. In the past year his letters had a strange quality about them, almost of madness, and Cardoza had been tempted to suggest he take a vacation. His research into the ancient lore of primitive tribes, once so stimulating, of late had appeared to have the opposite effect.

Montana broke the silence at last. "Rick, I have made a discovery you may not believe, but at least you must see and hear for yourself. If I am mad, then you are the only person I trust to help me. If I am not, then heaven help us both!"

Dr. Richard Cardoza stared at him in amazement. That first premonition he had experienced when a haggard Montana met him at the airport returned, and for an instant he wished that he were back in his laboratory in Tucson.

Apprehension swept over him as he realized that even if he had wanted to go back, it was too late, for there in the distance stood the mesa looming dark and enigmatic against an immense, storm-streaked sky. The place was unsettling enough in the daytime, but at night it became haunted and eerie.

Before them the Enchanted Mesa rose almost five hundred feet from the flat plain. The mesa top had been the home, centuries ago, of New Mexico's Acoma Indians before a tragic fate befell them.

To ensure safety from Apache attacks, villages were often built upon the top of mesas. They were, after all, natural fortresses. Fifteen hundred people had lived on top of the Mesa Encantada. Three hundred feet above the plain was a great opening like a cathedral arch, the entrance to a stair leading through a crevice in the rock and upward to the summit. From the plain to the arch was an outer stair of stone spiraling up the sides of a great column that leaned against the mesa.

Every day the young men came down from the mesa to the plain to work in the maize fields and to hunt. One afternoon the sky grew black. There were crashes of thunder, brilliant flashes of lightning, and heavy rain, so the men took shelter at the base of the mesa to wait until it passed over. As they sheltered themselves beneath the rock, there came a deafening crash of thunder and lightning, and stones began to fall all around them. In a few minutes the storm was over, and the men saw that the outer steps leading up the mesa had been struck and shattered off by the lightning.

They scrambled up as far as they could, then slid back in frustration. The people left on top began trying to descend, but their efforts were equally futile. As they realized that the only way that led down from the mesa was gone and there was no escape, they began to scream and weep. The best archers at the foot of the rocks could not send game far enough on their arrows to reach the top. The next day one woman, crazed by thirst, leaped down to her death, and on each succeeding day there were fewer faces staring down at the men below. Finally there were none, and those who were left at the base went to a mesa two miles away and built another home. They called it Acoma—city of the sky.

Joseph Montana parked his car near the foot of the Enchanted Mesa and motioned to the bewildered Cardoza to get out. He led him around the base until he

reached a rock from which they could see the top, climbed upon it, and beckoned to Cardoza to follow. "We'll wait here," he said staring upward at the mesa.

They sat there for more than an hour. Then Montana whispered, "Look up on top of the mesa. Do you see it?" Cardoza shook his head. Then a few minutes later he saw a small light. The light grew larger and larger, finally resembling a shining disc. The moon? Hardly, for there was a slight drizzle of rain and the sky was completely overcast. The lighted disc, which must have been as high as a house, rolled slowly toward the center of the mesa and then stopped. "Do you see it now?" asked Montana. Cardoza nodded. There was an oval area of darkness in the center, almost the shape of a door, and he was astonished to see several figures step out.

They appeared to be luminous, and, skeptical as he was, they looked like men. They walked about for a few minutes and then filed back into the disc. The disc grew so bright that he could hardly bear to watch, and it began to rise in the air. The light grew less brilliant, then smaller and smaller as it vanished into the night sky.

"Good heavens, man, what in the world was that?" asked Cardoza.

"You saw it, too, then? You don't think I'm crazy?"

"Of course I saw it. What a question! I saw the whole thing."

"You know it's strange that no human skeletons were ever found on top of the Enchanted Mesa," said Montana. "When it was finally scaled with ropes and other equipment by a government exploring party in

1897, they found proof of its ancient occupancy—chips and tools of stone, pieces of pottery, relics of masonry and part of the old broken-off trail. But they never found the skeleton of a man, woman or child? And it was the old people, the women, and the children who were marooned up there. They couldn't possibly have gotten down. There is no way to get people off the top of that mesa unless you had an army helicopter or something."

"Or *something*! Now you've hit on it. There had to be a way to airlift those people off the mesa top."

"But, hundreds of years ago? What are you saying?"

"What did you just see, Rick?" Dr. Cardoza was silent. He stared at the top of the mesa. "All right. I see what you mean, but why should they come back?"

"Great Scott, man. Am I supposed to have all the answers? Isn't what we've seen enough?"

"Yes, it certainly is, Joseph. Do you suppose that beings from another planet saw what had happened, took pity on those poor people and rescued them?"

"Rick, this is one thing I don't want to write any scholarly papers on, but I think that is exactly what happened!"

WILD BILL HICKOK
IN ABILENE

Abilene was the wildest cattle town in the West, the town where the saloon keepers wore diamonds as big as hickory nuts and kept six-shooters behind the bar, where at any time a drunken cowboy might ride his horse into a saloon, pull his pistol, and shoot in the air.

The Broadway of Abilene was Texas Street, which led right off the dreary prairie straight down a glittering path to hell itself. Drinking and gambling houses dotted both sides of the street—the Alamo, Lone Star, Long Horn, and Bull's Head.

When the cowboys rode into Abilene after three months of driving a herd of cattle across the prairie, they found themselves in glamorous surroundings where it was easy to raise Cain and blow their pay. For the gamblers there was a rich harvest in this Sin City, and it was not too unusual to see a hatful of gold or silver spread out on one of the gambling tables.

The town fathers hired Tom Smith, a former New York City policeman, as their first marshal, but he was murdered before he could tame the town. It was natural that they should hire a fast draw expert named Wild Bill Hickok to be the new marshal.

Strangely enough, a ghost was responsible for Wild Bill's leaving Abilene.

In the late 1860s Abilene was running wild; city ordinances were posted and just as quickly torn down. The blinds were ripped off the mayor's office, and cowboys rode through town shooting at the "no shooting" posters on the doors. When the town tried to build a jail, the cowboys demolished it. The first marshal had made a good start, but he was dead. Abilene was without a chief of police, and the town's reputation was so bad that no one wanted the job.

When Wild Bill Hickok presented himself, the mayor was glad to hire him. He was reputed to be the best gunman in all the West and was a crack shot with both hands at the same time.

The town was not entirely happy with the choice of a man they considered a desperado. Tall and striking in appearance, always well dressed, he attracted much attention and more than a little jealousy from most of the men.

But Smith had run things pretty well, and Wild Bill continued Smith's custom of having the cowboys park their weapons when they went in the saloons and gambling houses, and the fear of his two pistols kept many a roughneck in line. His office was in the Alamo saloon, and he employed an assistant or two to patrol the streets and watch for trouble.

Unfortunately Hickok had made some enemies as he enforced the law, and at the same time his growing reputation had made various gunmen eager to shoot him. At least eight thugs had come to Abilene to try it. Wild Bill disarmed seven of them who lost their courage. The eighth did not, and that is when Wild Bill met a ghost.

It happened this way. One night Wild Bill left his headquarters at the Alamo saloon and walked down the street toward the Merchant's Hotel when he saw a gunman come out of the shadows and start to draw on him. Wild Bill had an advantage over almost any gunman, and he drew and fired his pistol. The thug dropped to the ground. Before he died, he lifted his head and swore, "Wild Bill, I'm going to get even with you!" Nobody knew the gunman's name, and he was buried at Boot Hill in an unmarked grave.

The next night Hickok was walking down the street, and just as he approached the Merchant's Hotel, he saw a gunman in the shadows and then, as if time had begun to turn in slow motion, he had the feeling that this had already happened. The man even looked like the same man he had shot the night before, drawing in the same fashion. In a fast draw the gunman pulled his .44. At the last moment Wild Bill managed to break his trance, draw his guns, and blast away, expecting for the first time in his life that he was going to be shot. But all he heard were the reports of his own gun. Then he looked in amazement. He was still standing, and so was

the man he had shot. Nobody was down, and Wild Bill was astonished. The figure began to dissolve, feet first, and drifted away like a puff of smoke.

Wild Bill headed back to the Alamo, downed a double shot of whiskey, and told not a soul. The next night was a night history will remember as the night Wild Bill made his tragic mistake. His arch enemy, the gambler Phil Coe, who had sworn to kill him, led a gang of roughnecks down the street, and they stopped outside the door of the saloon. All the men had been drinking heavily, and Coe fired off his pistol.

Hickok rushed to the door to investigate and found Coe standing there arrogantly. "I only shot a dog," said Coe, "and if you want my gun, you'll have to take it!" With that Coe went for his pistol. Hickok drew both guns and fired. Coe's shot went wild, but a ball from one of Hickok's guns penetrated Coe's stomach, and he fell to the street mortally wounded.

At the same instant Hickok saw a figure approaching from the shadows looking ready to draw. Struck with fear, Wild Bill fired with his left hand almost instantly. He was sure he had seen that same awful face for the third time. But the figure slumped down. It was not "the gunman" he had shot but rather his fellow policeman and friend, Mike Williams.

When he saw what he had accidentally done, he was shocked. He went and got a preacher out of bed and brought him to the dying gambler's side to pray for him. Then he sadly made the arrangements for his friend's funeral, sent money to the mother to come to Abilene, purchased a fine casket, and shipped the body to Williams's home at Kansas City—paying the entire bill himself.

And that is how a gunman's ghost tricked Wild Bill Hickok into killing the wrong man, thus getting his evil revenge. Not long after that the town fathers urged Wild Bill to turn in his badge and move on.

The gunman's ghost was never seen again, but the grave is still up on Boot Hill.

THE PHANTOM RIDER OF
THE BUTTERFIELD STAGE

It was a gray, drizzly day in October of 1887. Bill Peets was a good stage driver, and he loved the short-grass country with its endless reaches of prairie. But on the last stretch toward Abilene he always whipped the horses into a frenzied gallop, for this was the area where bandits and Indians were likely to appear. Today he was carrying two passengers and the mail.

Peets was just about to bring the whip down hard on the backs of the lead horses when he saw a woman's figure standing near the trail in the rain. She raised her arm and waved desperately at the approaching stage. Peets yelled at his horses and dropped the wooden brake. With violent jerkings and bumpings, the stage lurched to a halt.

"What's going on, you triflin' cuss? You tryin' to throw us out of this here stage?" came a yell from within the coach.

"Hold on, I got to pick up a passenger," replied Peets. "Passenger? Ain't nothin' out here but prairie dogs and Indians."

The woman came up to the stage. "Can you take me to Abilene? My husband and I lost our way, and the wagon broke a wheel. I must find someone to go back and help him." Her dress was wet, her bonnet bedraggled and stained, but Peets noticed her face was still pretty despite her distress.

"Sure, always ready to help a lady," he replied, getting down and producing a blanket from beneath his seat. "Here, wrap this around you." He opened the door of the stage and introduced her to the tall, lean cowboy and the young banker from the East. The cowboy glanced at her in surprise. "Well, I don't mind bein' shaken up so much now, pardner, but we'd better get a move on or the next stop might be for Indians."

He moved his gear from the seat next to him and gallantly offered the lady some water. She shook her head. "Where you from, ma'am?" She pointed westward. What a hard life it was out here for a woman, he thought to himself. Probably the wife of some frontiersman who hoped to carve a ranch out of the miles of sand burrs, soap weeds, and cactus. The young banker lost interest in the new passenger and began to read an old paper from back east that he had found on the floor of the stage.

The name of the cowboy was Flood. He was a Texan who knew nothing but cattle, and he had been thinking about the herd he was to bring in from Mexico. He would soon be heading for the mouth of the Rio Grande to receive the cattle for delivery on an Indian reservation.

The lady settled herself with the blanket over her knees and stared out the window. She didn't seem eager to talk.

But the banker felt he had to give Flood some advice about cattlemen.

"Don't you know that that man you hired at our last stop is the worst drunkard in this country?"

"No, I didn't know that," replied Flood, "but I don't want to ruin an innocent man with a trail outfit. Just so the herd don't count out short on the day of delivery, I don't mind how many drinks the outfit takes."

The lady looked shocked, and the banker, irritated that his advice was taken so casually, turned back to his paper. In a little while he fell asleep and began to snore. The cowman excused himself to the lady saying he believed he'd go up front and sit with the driver. She nodded but didn't turn her head.

Peets and Flood traded stories, mostly talk about their exploits during Indian raids, and the time passed without incident. Both men understood each other and the country. Peets cursed the desert land and said, "Maybe when I die, it will kind of hurry the devil to find some punishment for me that I ain't already been used to from livin' in Kansas." Flood nodded in agreement.

The horses were going at a fast clip, and the stage was making good time; in fact they would be arriving in Abilene a little early. When they pulled in, Flood jumped down, going around to the lady's side to let her out. There sat the fancy, know-it-all banker from the East slumped over in the corner of his seat still snoring. But the seat across from him was empty! The woman was gone. The blanket was on the floor of the stage. Flood found it a little damp as he leaned over to pick it up. Under it was one small, muddied shoe.

Wide awake by now the banker called out, "What happened to her? Where is that woman we picked up? Did you let her off some place?"

"Like where?" answered Flood with disgust. "Ain't no place to let a woman off out there in the desert where we been tonight, much less a woman alone. What happened to her? You was the one in here with her."

The small, dapper man looked frightened. "What kind of a coach is this anyway?" he asked Peets. "You pick up women in the middle of nowhere, and you let them off in the middle of nowhere!" He scurried off toward one of the hotels.

Flood looked bewildered. "Peets, where you reckon that woman got to?" Peets picked up the small shoe. "You know, ladies ain't worn shoes like this in a long time. Look at that stain. That's not mud. Looks more like blood to me. Flood, it's my 'pinion we been ridin' with somethin' mighty strange tonight. If you'd care to join me for a bit a reinforcement at the Alamo saloon, I'm ready for it."

"You know, Peets, that woman didn't never take off her bonnet, and there was a stain on the side of her face just about the color a this 'un on the shoe. You think it was Indians that she got loose from?"

"I don't think she ever got loose. That warn't no real, live, flesh and blood woman we picked up tonight. That was a ghost, sure's you're livin'."

THE LOVELY APPARITION
OF FORT DAVIS

W hy should a lovely apparition haunt a desolate fort in Texas? The story is a strange one
and began about the time of the Civil War.
Across the West, from the Dakotas to the Texas border, from Kansas to California, are strung the forts that
were once brave outposts of a wild and lonely frontier,
manned by a courageous breed of men. There was Fort
Union in New Mexico, Fort Bowie in Arizona, Fort
Laramie in Wyoming, and in Texas, Fort Stockton and
Fort Davis. Many are the tales that have been told
about these forts, but among the most mysterious is a
story sometimes heard at Fort Davis.

Fort Davis was built as a warning to the Apaches,
a protection to travelers from San Antonio to El Paso,
and, if need be, a refuge for settlers in the event of

Indian attacks. The fort itself was never directly attacked, but the coaches operating on the route through Fort Davis were often attacked by Indians.

Surrounded by a cloud of dust from the hooves of their galloping ponies, they would suddenly dash from behind a rock formation or out of a canyon. With horrifying cries and fiercely painted faces, they fell upon the unwary. Some passengers were lucky enough to reach Fort Davis; others were murdered.

The construction of Fort Davis was primitive, for at first it was planned to replace the buildings at a later time. Made of pine slabs set upright in the ground, they had plank or earth-packed floors, roofs of thatched grass or canvas, and glazed windows. There were thirteen houses for married soldiers and their families, a hospital, a stable, a store, and a billiards room. There were some compensations for this rough life—beautiful scenery, fresh water from Limpia Creek, and a large vegetable garden for the garrison.

There were also parties and social events for the officers and their wives and families. One of the loveliest young women at the fort was Alice Walpole, the wife of a young lieutenant from Alabama. She was often homesick, missing the blue-green hills and beautiful rivers of her home state.

After a long harsh winter in this arid country she found herself filled with longing for the southern spring. She began to think that even in this bleak countryside, somewhere roses might even now be in bloom. Alice decided to find them, and wrapping herself in a long blue wool cape, she left the house on officers' row, passed the post garden, and headed toward the mountains.

She had always felt tiny and insignificant beside the immense, foreboding mountains and the great stretches of open, empty, desertlike land—the size of one of the calm-faced china dolls she had played with as a child. And, indeed, this land was often hostile. She continued to walk toward the mountains following Limpia Creek, for she had read that there were beautiful white roses blooming in the wilderness beyond the fort.

Alice never returned—at least not in human form. A party of soldiers from the fort spent several days searching for her while her young husband was filled with apprehension, then despair. The search party could find no trace of the girl.

Late one night a few months later a beautiful young woman was seen walking down the long row of officers' houses. The west wind blew her cape about her, and when she was greeted by a lieutenant who saw her, he could hardly be sure she replied, for her voice seemed to float away from him on the wind. There was something familiar about her. He turned to follow, thinking she might need assistance, only to have her vanish around the corner of one of the houses. The officer called out, but there was no answer, only the chill night wind flinging his words back to him. Then he realized the reason he had turned to follow this woman. She was Alice Walpole!

When the lovely apparition returned, she seemed always to seek out the quarters where the southern wives were socializing. And so, far from the red clay soil of her native Alabama, this girl with the west wind blowing her ghostly cape sometimes came back to seek companionship.

She never actually spoke, and the most tangible evidence of her presence was a sudden strong fragrance of roses in a room or a few wild white roses mysteriously left here or there.

One day in 1861 after word of the start of the Civil War had reached Fort Davis, seven of the young southern officers called at the commandant's office with letters of resignation before heading east to offer their services to the Confederacy. General Twiggs, who was now less worried about Indians than about the demand from the State of Texas to surrender his fort, noticed in the midst of it all a vase of white roses on his desk.

As the officers one by one presented their letters of resignation it is said that he later commented, "Seven white roses, seven resignations—what a coincidence!"

The ghost of the lost girl was not seen during the war years as far as anyone knows. Perhaps it departed with the southern officers and their wives. Later, when southerners once more returned to Fort Davis, her ghost reappeared. It was most often glimpsed in the quarters of the lonely and sometimes homesick young women. And the presence of the lovely Alice is always suspected whenever a white rose is found.

PANCHO VILLA'S TREASURE
AND THE GHOST CAT

He awoke shivering with terror, perspiration pouring from him. The room was pitch black; the lamp he had left burning in his hotel room before retiring had gone out. Yet he was certain he was not alone. Something too horrible to imagine was in the room with him. His mouth was dry. He was too petrified even to scream. Something began to move on the bed near him, and straining to see, he found himself looking into two glowing, baleful yellow eyes. Leaping from his bed, he dashed outside the room, feeling his very soul was in danger from this evil presence.

He was not the first nor would he be the last guest to be frightened nearly out of his senses at the Fort Stockton Hotel. But we are getting ahead of our story.

Eugene Webber had slept in a bedroll on the plains under the stars. He had dozed fitfully as a wagon rolled along in the darkness. Now the thin, gray-faced little man stood before the square, dust-colored adobe building that was Fort Stockton's first hotel and stared at it thoughtfully. A large cat purred and rubbed against his legs.

Webber went in to the desk to register. "I have only one room left. How long will you be wanting it?" asked the weather-beaten middle-aged woman who stared at him curiously. "I'll try it by the week for a while, ma'am," he replied. He was wearing a gun belt but certainly did not look like a gunman, so she handed a key over to him. She had been in the West long enough to tag her guests pretty quickly, but this man puzzled her.

"Eugene Webber," she watched him write on the register. Then she looked down at the cat near his feet. "Mr. Webber, is that your cat?" Webber paused for a moment staring at the animal as it rubbed affectionately about his legs. He hesitated. He had never seen the cat before. But he replied, "Yes, I guess it is. Don't worry about him. I'll see that he doesn't give you any trouble."

"It's not my habit to let guests keep animals, Mr. Webber, we'll see."

"He'll stay in my room and not bother anybody," her new guest promised.

Webber glanced quickly around the lobby. The hotel appeared to be comfortable and safe. Safe—that was the main thing. Fort Stockton was a railroad town, which meant that it had a better hotel than most, and the countryside around it was so flat and bare a fox could scarcely have found cover.

Hotels like this brought together all sorts of people since they were often the only places to eat, drink, and sleep. All of life was acted out here—birth, marriage, death—and for many the hotels became permanent homes. Misfits from the more civilized parts of the country found these hotels a convenient place to live and to die.

Webber had a corner room, small, probably about ten by fourteen feet, but it was comfortable and it looked out over a courtyard full of small trees and flowering shrubs. He stood in his doorway for a moment admiring the desert willow in bloom, stroking the cat, and then with a faint, satisfied smile, he closed the door. Unbuckling his ammunition belt, he hung it on a nail. It was an unusual belt, more Spanish than western in style. He removed the revolver, set the safety catch, and, with the weapon in his hand, Gene Webber turned over and went to sleep.

When he awoke, it was time for dinner. The cat lay curled on the bed beside him. "Mr. Whiskers. How's that for a name? I don't know what you and me are doing here together, but you stick with old Webber and you'll be livin' in clover, or whatever cats like to live in." He gave Mr. Whiskers a farewell pat on the head and went to supper.

Gene Webber kept to himself, and nobody at the hotel paid much attention to him. He paid promptly each week, and sometimes the lady who ran the hotel wondered where his money came from. She would try to draw him out in conversation, talking about claims and how some men struck it rich and others didn't, but Webber never made any comment. If the question was a direct one, he just acted as if he hadn't heard her.

In the evening Webber would sit on the bench on the porch with Mr. Whiskers sitting beside him. In the morning he would walk down to some of the stores. Children liked him for he was always giving them a piece of rock candy or some small treat. Week after week went by, and the sight of Webber and the cat sunning in the little courtyard or of the two of them walking down the street, the cat following, was accepted. Characters came and went in the frontier towns, and soon no one thought much about Webber except to sometimes speculate idly about the fact that although he never left Fort Stockton or seemed to do any work, he always had money.

After Webber had been there for about a month, a half-dozen blood-thirsty-looking characters arrived at the Fort Stockton Hotel about suppertime and demanded to be served. They were obviously Mexicans, probably outlaws. At first it appeared they were going to rob the guests in the dining room. They cursed and yelled and insulted everyone in sight, and in the confusion Webber slipped out. Pancho Villa's payroll had been stolen, and the Mexicans were determined to find and string up the culprit. They were so ready to make trouble that most of the guests lost their appetites and left the dining room hurriedly. The Mexicans were unable to find the man they sought.

Weeks turned into months and months into years. One day Webber did not appear for any of his meals. His landlady went to investigate and knocked several

times but received no answer. One of the men helped her force open the door, and there lay Webber on the bed—dead. His hand still grasped his gun. Strangely enough, Mr. Whiskers was nowhere to be seen. There was much discussion about notifying relatives, but no one knew who they were.

Some said that he was wealthy and had hidden a treasure in the walls or the floor, but no one dared to arouse the wrath of the landlady by damaging the walls or taking up the floorboards. Within a few days the room was rented again. A short time later several of the guests complained that they had been awakened in the middle of the night by something springing on their bed and trying to claw them. Several claimed to have seen the vicious yellow eyes of a huge cat, its shadowy form lunging at them. One evening a man sitting on the bench facing the street suddenly leaped into the air with a wild scream, crying out that he had sat on a cat and been clawed. But his friends laughed uproariously, saying he had been "clawed by too much strong drink" at a nearby bar.

On a hot summer night about a month after Webber's death, two Mexicans rode into town. They stopped at the Fort Stockton Hotel and told the landlady that the man who had stolen Pancho Villa's payroll lived there and they had come to get him and the gold. They described her former guest, and when she told them he was dead, the men became livid with rage and demanded to see his room. She showed them the room, and they searched it but found nothing. While they were there, the town marshal appeared, and the men left.

By now the landlady was convinced that her mysterious guest had undoubtedly stolen the payroll and outwitted Pancho Villa himself. She tapped the walls searching for hollow places. She looked for loose boards in the floor but could find none. Several years later when the worn, old floor was replaced, the workmen were surprised to find a skeleton.

The local doctor identified it as the bones of a very large cat. Everyone was certain it was Webber's close companion, Mr. Whiskers. Even with the interment of the cat's skeleton, now and then late at night a guest would scream in terror and dash out of Webber's old room into the courtyard. Some maintained they had been attacked by a being so vicious it must surely have come from hell itself. Was it Mr. Whiskers, the mild-mannered Webber, or the angry ghost of Pancho Villa that continued to haunt the room in the old Fort Stockton Hotel?

THE GHOST OF
CRIPPLE CREEK

D o dry bones rise again? Perhaps. And if they do, it will be at Cripple Creek.

It was late at night, and the couple that stood in the moonlight staring curiously through the window of the old gold assay office were alone on the street. "Wait a minute," said the young man as he put his arm about the waist of his girl and drew her toward the window. "Do you see anything in there?"

"No," answered the girl, "and neither do you. Just because your grandfather once lived here, I don't see why you get so excited about this town. It looks like something out of the late 1890s to me."

"You're right. And that's what fascinates me," said the young man. "Look through the window." In the dim light within they could see boxes piled everywhere,

ASSAY OFFICE

bottles of chemicals still on the shelves, even a mortar and pestle on the counter. Why were these things still here? The assay office had been closed for a very long time.

"Keep looking over there toward the counter, and I think you will see something really incredible."

The girl stopped smiling and stood quietly straining to see into the office, which was lighter than one might think since there was some illumination from the corner street lamp. Then her hand grasped his arm so tightly he almost cried out. Her face had turned as white as if she had seen a ghost, and she had!

Cripple Creek, high in the Colorado Rockies, had been the biggest gold-rush camp of them all. Here the last great gold rush moved from the reality of the prospector's pick to the bank vaults of the East, creating a city of hotels, bars, stores full of miner's supplies, an assay office, and even a trolley line to connect all the gold camps. Life here was harsh, often violent, and death no stranger to man, woman, or child, for if it did not come from the sharp report of a gun, disease was a killer, too.

But it was in the assay office that a miner's hopes were most often dashed. Although they were occasionally raised to the wild and dizzying heights of Pikes Peak. To assay ore is a complicated, exacting process, and while it is taking place, the prospector can indulge himself in a nearby bar or wait in the office to hear the words that will make him rich or return him to poverty. He never knows in advance whether he will toss the ore away in disgust or take those same samples and show them to a well-groomed man in a fashionable eastern-cut suit in one of the richly appointed railroad cars that dot the sidings along the tracks.

Here the wealthy wheel and deal and wait to buy the claims of the poor as they have always done. Often they haggle and dicker for diggings, acquiring them for a few thousand dollars when later they will produce millions. Of course they take the risk, but they would often discourage the naive miner from retaining even a small share in his claim.

It was October of 1899. Dust blew down the streets, the wind tossed along an occasional aspen leaf, and winter was on its way to Cripple Creek. After two years of disappointment and hard luck, Jake Jernigan was ready for a break. His bare little shack with its cracks was scarcely better than some of the tents, but he was sure he was digging near the mother lode.

How much longer he would be able to get credit from old man Warren to buy food, he didn't know. If Jeannie hadn't had plenty of gumption and love for him, she wouldn't have stayed—but would she continue to take it? The last week or so he had even begun to wonder about himself. He had developed a painful, hacking cough that never seemed to leave him.

This morning he watched Jeannie trying to find enough food for his lunch bucket, and he felt more discouraged than he could remember, but he tried not to let her see it. Walking along through the sagebrush and mounds of granite among the diggings heading toward his own claim on Mineral Hill, he was still convinced that this was where the mother lode would be discovered. When he reached his claim, he began chipping away with his pick. All day long he attacked the stubborn rock, pausing only during the fits of coughing. His shoulders began to ache, and perspiration streaked his face under the shapeless old felt hat.

Now the sun slid lower in the sky. Jernigan continued to batter the rock as if he could force it to yield him its treasure. The last rays of sunlight struck the ledge. And then he could scarcely believe it, for exposed to his wondering eyes was a wide, sparkling vein of the most beautiful ore he had ever seen.

A wild delight surged through him. He felt like a boy again. He wanted to shout, to leap high in the air, to run to town and tell Jeannie. The months of hard work and the miserable little house had all been worth it! With a few quick strokes of his pick he chipped off more ore to carry back. He would have to take it to the assayer to be certain, and many a miner had thought he had made a rich strike only to be bitterly disappointed.

Walking along Bennett Avenue to the assay office, his step was as springy as when he'd been on his way to court Jeannie before they were married. A horse and wagon clattered past him throwing up a cloud of dust. Ordinarily he might have shouted an imprecation at the driver, but he only gritted his teeth and spat out the dust.

He opened the door of the assay office with one hand—his pick and lunch bucket in the other—conscious of the heavy ore weighing down the pocket of his old jacket. There stood the assayer, ready to close, putting away his equipment. A flood of disappointment and frustration swept over Jernigan, and he lunged toward the counter. The assayer's eyes looked frightened. He had seen many a man become violent over gold.

Then the assayer recognized Jernigan, and his fear turned to relief.

"What the devil do you mean scaring a fellow by comin' at him like that? I'm all ready to leave on a trip." Jernigan leaned across the counter, his face desperate, "Look, you and me been knowin' each other a long time. Run this ore for me before you leave, please. This time I've really struck it. I know I have."

The assayer's face relaxed into a faint, tired smile. For the few who struck it rich here, there were many who lost everything but their wild dreams—dreams that often wrecked them and their families. But he liked Jernigan and had even begun to feel sorry for him. Suppose he did have some good news for him, just suppose. It could change the man's whole life. The ore did look interesting. Stretching out his hand, he said, "Oh, all right, Jernigan. Let's see what you've got this time."

To assay ore is an exacting process, but Jernigan sat down to wait. The words the assayer would speak could make him rich or poor.

The assayer crushed the ore and then bent absorbed over his tests. The miner studied his face hoping for some clue. Now the assayer was frowning. All the worry of the past few months seemed to crowd back in upon him, and Jernigan's chest felt tight. He must have made some sound for the other man glanced up sympathetically.

"Was that you sighing?"

"Guess it was."

"Things really that bad, Jernigan?"

Jernigan tried to reply but began to cough instead, the harsh, racking cough that had bothered him so much of late. The assayer stared at him thoughtfully for a moment. Then he took his pen in hand. It would be so easy to turn a one into a nine. His hand paused for a moment then wrote quickly across the paper. A smile lit up his face as if he had just peeked behind a curtain into the next world and found the streets there made of solid gold.

"Jernigan, you were right. This is the richest ore I've seen in many a day. These samples assay at over nine hundred dollars per ton!" Jernigan was stunned. The assayer came around from behind the counter, seized his arm, and began dancing him about the room.

"Don't you understand? You're rich, Jernigan!" A grin appeared on the miner's face, and then he, too, began to dance and jump wildly about shouting and laughing. Anyone passing by would have thought the two drunk, very drunk indeed. Pocketing the report, Jernigan went out the door. The buildings of Cripple Creek spun as he came out of the office.

Later that night when he left the fine railroad car and made his way home, he was fifteen thousand dollars richer than he had been that morning. He had been talked out of keeping any share in the claim, but maybe that was just as well, for Jeannie and he ought to be back east on their own farm. Now he had the money to buy it.

One morning a few days later, when Jeannie had just finished the packing, she heard a loud knock at the door. When she opened it, she saw a hard-faced man dressed in expensive clothes.

"Your husband played me for a fool, woman. Give me the money back." Jeannie stared at him, not understanding.

"That claim of his was worthless, worthless, do you hear me?" He began to shout angrily. A voice spoke up from the road, a friend of her husband's who was a deputy. He looked at the man coldly.

"Get out and don't ever come back, you greedy rat. That was probably the first claim you didn't cheat some poor miner out of. Now don't ever bother this lady again, or some night when you're needin' help out there at that fine railroad car, there won't be nobody to come. Nobody at all! Do you understand?"

The man's face turned pale. He started to reply but thought better of it and left. That afternoon Jake and Jeannie rode out of the brick depot at the head of Bennett Avenue and left Cripple Creek behind forever.

Staring into the old assay office, the couple's eyes were wide and incredulous. For there in the shadows in front of the counter were two figures whirling around in a delirious sort of dance. Leaping, jumping, arm in arm they cavorted together. And as each, in turn, faced momentarily toward the window, the couple saw the chalk-white, bony, grotesquely grinning faces of a pair of skeletons.

Not all ghosts are created by moments of sadness. Sometimes it may be a moment of intense joy. And so it is that even many years later in an old assay office, there are nights when the dead live again at Cripple Creek!

THE RIDER WORE
A GREEN HABIT

"You are out of your mind if you think you are leaving Virginia to go with me, Emma," said Edward Dobbs. "The American Fur Trading Company is sending me to manage a remote trading post way out in Wyoming. I cannot take care of a headstrong daughter like you out there."

"I want to be with you, Father. Not stay here in the East with Aunt Lily. I was the best rider at school; you don't have to worry about me. Watch me," she said, and with that she galloped off on her beautiful black stallion, Midnight. His heart almost stopped as he saw the horse approach a tumultuous stream at the edge of the pasture, sail over it, and dash out of sight. But in a moment the girl and the horse reappeared and were galloping back toward him. His daughter's small green hat sat jauntily atop the black hair streaming out behind her, and her green dress flowed in the wind—the outfit became her he thought.

Educated at Chatham Hall, one of the finest girls' schools in Virginia, Emma was her father's pride and joy. She was the image of her mother, who had died ten days after Emma's birth. He had not remarried. They lived with his twin sister, Lily, who had taken care of Emma since infancy and was also her severest critic at times.

"I am concerned about Emma," she told her brother, "for she is a very headstrong girl. The wise see danger and take refuge, but the inexperienced head right into it and suffer for it."

"Where did you get that, Lily?"

"From the book of Proverbs. The Bible has kept me out of a great deal of trouble, Edward. I have raised her in the church, and Emma knows right from wrong, but she is willful, Edward," warned his sister.

Gradually Emma prevailed, as she knew she would —and as she always had with her father since her mother's death—by making fervent promises to obey him.

"I think she will bear up well under the trip for she is an excellent rider, and she has promised me she will not leave the fort alone," her father told Lily.

Edward Dobbs and his daughter, Emma, left a few days later on what was to prove a wild and dangerous journey deep into the Wyoming wilderness. There were narrowly averted brushes with Indians and nights that filled Emma with terror at the unfamiliar sounds of wild animals. The most fearful of all to her was the howling of the wolves.

When they finally arrived, she was shocked to find that their destination had been this small, primitive log-walled cottonwood building at the meeting of the Laramie and North Platte rivers. How could her father have brought her to this dreadful, desolate place out here in the middle of nowhere? There were no trees about the fort to protect it from the heat of the sun reflected from the surrounding hills—just the bright enormous sky overhead that made her feel like a tiny speck. She began to forget her entreaties and the promises she had made to her father and to think longingly of home back east.

In 1850 Fort Laramie was run by the American Fur Trading Company, which had bought the post to trade furs with the Sioux and Cheyenne nations.

"See all the people heading out here from the East," her father said. "This is going to become the first major American outpost on the western plains."

The 1840s had seen thousands of hardy pioneers walking, rolling handcarts, or in long wagon trains on the Oregon Trail. And now there came a constant stream of gold prospectors from the Midwest and the South. Emma was astonished to see wagons of all patterns, sizes, and descriptions drawn by bulls, cows, oxen, mules, and horses. It was estimated that between thirty to fifty thousand people followed the trail west.

Emma watched the Indians crowd around the fort to trade. She saw quite a few Indian women—the wives of traders and trappers—and their children lounging about the fort. They sat in doorways, their brown eyes filled with curiosity as they stared at her.

"Those people are from the Sioux tribe," said her father, and he began talking with Mr. Husband, the manager of the post, as he watched men stow and pack buffalo robes and skins.

"Do they have food here at the post?" Emma asked her father.

"Most of the food they have is jerked buffalo meat," he replied, "and you will have ample opportunity to try that." Emma made a face.

"You may learn to like it," he said with a faint smile. "Look, here is a letter deposit. For twenty-five cents you can send a letter to the States to Aunt Lily."

"When will we be going back to the States, Father?"

"In about a year—or perhaps sooner," he added. He had become more strict about her leaving the fort since Indian problems had begun to develop, but her father did not share all of this with Emma for he did not wish to alarm her. She treated the Indian braves who came and went bringing furs with a casual friendliness that he was not sure they understood, and her father was well aware of their long admiring looks. He realized she had no idea of the dangerous impulses of these men.

In 1849 the U.S. government had purchased the post and began building Laramie up as an important military garrison. The purpose was to protect travelers from both Indians and bandits. Every day brought new scenes and fresh excitement. Fort Laramie was serving as a stage station, Pony Express stop, and a getting-off place for all kinds of men.

Emma soon began to enjoy the daily excitement at Laramie. She made a striking figure as she rode about the fort in her beautiful green riding dress with a tiny green hat perched on her dark hair. But inwardly she chaffed at the promise she had made her father that she would never leave the safety of the fort without an escort of his assistants. A naive young woman brought up in a much more civilized part of this new world, she failed to understand why her father would order her to stay in the environs of the fort when he knew she was an excellent rider. She could outrun anyone on Midnight, she told herself. Finally the only thing that kept her from galloping away from the fort without her escorts, for at least a brief ride alone, was the thought of the eerie howling of the wolves that sometimes awakened her at night.

Believing her father's rule was silly, one day when he was called away from the post to nearby Fort Platte, Emma rode out alone. Her father's men did not see her at first. Then one of them spotted the figure of the girl some distance out on the plain. Dressed in her green riding habit with a jaunty green hat perched on her black hair, she was galloping at top speed on her black stallion, Midnight. The men whose responsibility it was to escort her gave desperate chase, but her lead was too great and soon she was only a tiny dot on the horizon.

Gradually the men straggled back to the fort, believing she would return soon. Some of them shook their heads as dusk fell and the wolves began to howl. Her father galloped up to the fort after dark, and his solemn-faced employees greeted him. He set out to find Emma with two of the men who knew the country well, but they returned without her. There were countless reports that a girl in a green riding habit was seen here and there along the Oregon Trail, sometimes galloping with her hair flowing out behind her, but the heartbroken father never saw his daughter again and finally became convinced that she had been killed by wild animals or at the hands of Indians on the prowl for stray scalps.

Although many believe they have seen the apparition of the girl over the years, the first recorded sighting of the "Lady in Green" came twenty years later. In 1871 Lieutenant James Nicholas Allison, a West Point graduate, was stationed at Fort Laramie. Shortly after he arrived, he joined some of the other men in a wolf hunt. An excellent rider on a good mount, he found himself ahead of the other men. A young woman riding a black stallion at breakneck speed would soon intersect his path.

She wore a long green riding dress and a matching hat. With a flick of her wrist she cracked her whip across the flank of her horse, and her steed bounded across in front of him. He turned to follow this wild female rider only to find that she had vanished with no trace of hoof prints or further sightings.

The young officer rode out on many an afternoon following this experience, but he never saw this beautiful reckless girl again. Allison told his story to his commanding officer. He suggested that in the opinion of the men on the post the lady in green was the ghost of Edward Dobbs's daughter, who is seen occasionally even today.

INDIANS WHO
WON'T STAY DEAD

It was a hot July evening in 1882 when the two prospectors decided to make camp just west of the Pecos River. The pair had been out for almost a month alone, and after they settled down under the shade of a mesquite, they began to cook their supper.

Suddenly they happened to look up the desolate Pecos Valley, and on the horizon was a sight to make their blood run cold—Indians on horseback! It couldn't be! Indians had been cleared out of there almost twenty-five years before. Their attention had been so glued to the Indians that they almost failed to notice that coming from the opposite direction was a military provision wagon train guarded by a few soldiers.

Joe said, "We got to warn 'em. Them Indians are goin' to attack that wagon train, Clem." The two men mounted their mules, rifles in hand, and headed for the wagon train. It was odd that the train came right on, never slowing, as if the driver didn't see them at all. Joe and Clem could see the drivers cracking their whips.

When they were a little closer, Clem shouted out, "Apaches! Apaches!" Still there was no response. The wagons went right on lickety-split with the Indians galloping straight toward them. Joe and Clem watched in amazement. Then the wagons ground to a sudden halt, and just as the Indians had surrounded them, the canvas sides flew up, the backs opened and out poured dozens of blue-coated soldiers.

Clem saw an Apache coming straight for him. He lifted his Winchester and fired right into the ferocious painted face. It was as if the bullets were traveling through tumbleweed, for they made no impact at all! On came the horseman. Terrified, Clem bent to reload. When he looked up, the Indian had vanished, the wagon train was gone, and the night was still as death.

"Clem, have I been sittin' here on this old mule dreamin'?"

His partner was busy looking for the emergency liquor bottle brought along in the event of snake bite. "Heck no, you ain't been dreamin'. I never saw so many Indians in my life, and we're getting out of here. There's better places to camp in hell itself! I'm headin' on back to Langtry."

They rode all night and late the next afternoon were banging on the door of the Texas Rangers station on the dusty street of Langtry. After they had told their story to the ranger, who was convinced the two shaken prospectors were telling the truth, the ranger asked,

"When did you say this happened?"

"Yesterday."

"Well, you boys have got the two slowest mules in Texas, for that battle was fought twenty-five years ago in July of 1857. Lieutenant Hartz outwitted those Apaches by putting all his men into wagons and pretending to be a provision train on the way to Fort Davis. That's how the Apaches were finally cleared out of this area. Fact is, I've got an old newspaper account here in my desk somewhere. Yeah, here it is, that's right, it happened just twenty-five years ago yesterday."

"Clem, have you got that receipt for our supplies when we started off a month ago? You just look at that date and tell me what it is?" Clem pulled out the slip and there it was. "Well, we bought our supplies in June of '82, so how could we see a battle that was fought twenty-five years before?"

"You fellows aren't the first to come in with a story about Apaches out there," said the ranger. "Ten years ago our marshal sent a posse after those Indians, and you know what they found? They searched that entire area for two days and didn't find a thing—not a trace of an Apache. Some folks say that place is really haunted."

THE GHOST LIGHT OF MARFA

The Indians had seen it gleaming long years ago, and even today there are few people in Alpine and Marfa, Texas, who have not seen the ghost light.

Before the turn of the century, when cattlemen drove their herds to the railroad at Alpine, the cowboys used the mysterious Marfa light as their guide. When they saw it, they knew the stockyards were just twenty miles away.

"I first saw that light back in 1921," says Lee Plumbley of Marfa.

"I was driving along late at night and was still about forty miles from home. There it was in the sky ahead of me, in front of the Chinati Mountains. It gave off a soft glow, and at first I thought it must be a campfire somewhere up there in the mountains. But as I drove on, I didn't seem to be getting any closer to it. At first it appeared to be one light, but as I watched it, it would separate into two lights and then merge back again into one.

"My next thought was that it must be a window in some mountain cabin, but finally I realized that it would be impossible for a light in a window never to either get any closer or fade away as I drove. That was only the first of many times during the past fifty years that I've seen it so plain that it often lasts until dawn."

What causes the light? When did it first begin to shine? How long ago was it first seen? These are questions many people ask.

Mrs. Plumbley's parents, the Robert R. Ellisons, caught their first glimpse of the mysterious light in 1883 on their second night in Marfa. Robert Ellison didn't know where the light came from or why, but he often saw it and became very irritated with later skeptics who suggested that it was automobile headlights.

"When I came out here in 1883, automobiles in this country were pretty damned scarce," joked Ellison. In those days he first thought it was an Apache campfire, and he often used to search the countryside on horseback. He finally began to realize it was neither a campfire nor a homestead.

Ellison was a cattleman, and when he unloaded his cattle at what is now the town of Alpine and began driving them west toward Marfa, he would watch for the ghost light. "When they came through Paisano Pass," says Ellison's daughter, Mrs. Julia Plumbley,

"and began driving the cattle over the flats, they could see for long distances, for the air was very clear. It was along here that they would catch their first glimpse of the light and know they were not far from home."

Lee Plumbley has never experienced the slightest fear of the phenomenon. "To me, it has always been a friendly light. When you are out at night in this country, the towns and houses are far apart. When you've ridden for miles your first view of the light becomes a friendly thing, like coming upon a homestead and seeing a lighted window. It's a welcome, familiar sight."

Many theories have been advanced to explain it, and one has been that it is the phosphorescent illumination given off by swamp gas. Plumbley smiles at that. "There are no swamp areas around here. Why, the nearest river is the Rio Grande, and it's sixty miles to the south." Scientists have often come to investigate and solve the mystery and so far have gone away empty handed. "The best place to see it is to take Highway 90 from Alpine to Marfa and stop at the overpass," say the Plumbleys.

It would seem that the light has been seen since the arrival of the first settlers. A former sheriff of the county, Joe Bunton, was born here in 1887, and the light was "like a friend" to him. Bunton, who died a few years ago, used to say, "I lived down in the Chinati country, and when I rode into Marfa, I saw that light many a night. I used to take care of all that country on horseback. There just weren't any roads up there."

Sometimes the ghost light is seen to glow as softly as a star, then it will brighten until it becomes like a spotlight, then dim and fade away.

"The other night it was very near and very bright," says Mrs. Georgie Lee Kahl, manager of Marfa's Paisano Motel. "Sometimes it seems to be far off in the mountains and sometimes very near. It's about twenty miles to the foothills of the Chinati where we see the ghost light."

During World War II her husband, Fritz Kahl, was stationed at the now abandoned Marfa Army Air Field. He was an instructor there from 1943 until 1945, and the airmen at the base often tried to find the ghost light. They would try to triangulate it. It gave them something to do when they flew at night. They would fly in the direction they saw it only to find that it was behind them or in front of them. The men used to say it was like chasing a rainbow. They would bomb the light with sacks of flour and fly low over the mountains to locate the white areas the next day. But they never found any fissures in the earth, signs of campfires, houses, or roads—just the desolate, sun-baked Chinati Mountains.

Several years ago four surveyors were determined to track the light to its source. They took their surveying equipment and spent months in the effort, but to no avail. Back in the summer of 1918 cowboys decided they would find it, and they rode all over the mountains looking for it, but they had no luck. Nor have any other expeditions, although they have advanced theories from UFOs to the shining of the moon upon an undiscovered mica vein. The latter has been challenged since the mountains have been combed so thoroughly that it is probable a large, exposed lode would have been discovered years ago. This scarcely explains why the light shines brightly on dark and moonless nights.

And so, as you sit somewhere reading this story, the ghost light continues to gleam between the small towns of Marfa and Alpine, Texas, baffling the best efforts of science to lay its mysterious glow to rest.

THE SACRED EARTH
AT CHIMAYÓ

Many will travel the winding road to Chimayó, and some will never be the same again. Each year thousands of people visit the chapel in this Spanish village of northern New Mexico in search of a miracle.

It is said that the earth found in a pit in a small room of El Santuario de Chimayó has great healing powers—powers that can cure pain, rheumatism, sadness, and paralysis. According to Indian legend, the site of the beautiful chapel was once a shrine, but no one knows how the earth here received its curative power.

Long ago Chimayó was a place where fire, smoke, and immense columns of boiling water and steam issued from the ground. Then only a pool of water was left, and it became a healing, hot mud spring atop Black

Mesa. From the most ancient times this valley of Chimayó was inhabited by Indians.

Years later, when the Spaniards came, they tried to Christianize these Indians, and there was a very kind and devout priest who traveled about the countryside carrying with him a large cross. But the Indians resented the cruel treatment they had endured at the hands of the Spanish soldiers, and one day, as the priest was walking along near the town of El Potrero, some Indians killed the poor man. The Spaniards found his body and buried it along with the large cross he carried.

In the early part of the nineteenth century the Santa Cruz River overflowed its banks and then receded. Shortly afterward, during Holy Week, Bernardo Abeyeta, a devout member of a religious group called the Penitentes, was walking through the hills of Potrero and was astonished to see a bright light shining from a spot near the Santa Cruz River. He rushed to the place and began to dig with his bare hands. Buried in the earth was a large and shining cross with the figure of the crucified Christ. Bernardo took the crucifix back to his village and began showing it to everyone. The people decided their own village was too humble a place for such a beautiful crucifix and that it should be taken to nearby Santa Cruz. So they organized a procession and carried the cross to Santa Cruz, placing it in the niche over the main altar of the church.

The next morning the crucifix was gone. A search was made, and the cross was found in the same hole where it had first been discovered. Another procession was formed to take it back to Santa Cruz, but the same thing happened. A third time it was taken to Santa

Cruz, and again it mysteriously returned to El Potrero. This was taken as a sign that the cross wished to remain in El Potrero, and the people of the village, led by Bernardo Abeyeta, began to build a church over the hole where the cross had been found.

The hole where he had found the crucifix and over which the chapel was built was the same pit of mud the Indians believed had healing powers, and Bernardo had great faith in the miraculous powers of this earth. Unfortunately, after his death in 1856 no one remained who seemed to know the real reason for the shrine, and many stories were invented, some connecting it with the Christ Child.

But the reputation of the healing power of the earth persisted, and pilgrims continued to visit the shrine. Among them was a little girl, Maria Martinez, who had been ill with a serious disease. Her mother made a vow that, if Maria recovered, she would make a pilgrimage here to give thanks. Maria recovered, and they visited the chapel. While little Maria rubbed herself with the sacred earth, her mother offered fervent prayers to the Christ Child. Many years later this little girl became the famed potter of San Ildefonso Pueblo north of Santa Fe.

In front of the church stands an ancient cottonwood tree, which was there in the days of Bernardo Abeyeta. A few yards away flows a beautiful, clear stream. Hollyhocks bloom beside the chapel's adobe walls, and though tourists come and go, it is a quiet, reverent atmosphere. Sunlight sifts through the cottonwood leaves upon the front of the chapel, turning El Santuario de Chimayó a glowing rose color. At the same time there is an expectant quality in the air. For as each pilgrim carries his pain, whether of body or of spirit, into the little room at the rear of the chapel and touches himself with the earth, there is the feeling that something exciting is happening here and that it may happen again tomorrow, next year, or a century from now.

THE HAUNTED
KIMO THEATER

Many American immigrants arrived in this country with magnificent dreams, and Oreste Bachechi was one of them. He began his business career in a tent and some twenty years later built a flamboyant southwestern theater building in Albuquerque, New Mexico.

He cleverly combined the fashionable art deco look of the day with that of an Indian pueblo. Unfortunately Bachechi died within a year after achieving his dream, and he never saw the famous stars who would play there in later years.

The theater was named "KiMo," a combination of two Indian words that mean "king of its kind." To go to a movie there was an event for families, and to be allowed to attend with friends was a coming of age experience for children.

When Bobby Darnall begged his family to allow him to go with a group of friends from his school, he was only six and younger than the others. His parents were reluctant because the boy was sensitive and easily frightened during movies. Sometimes his father would see something scary coming up on the screen and quickly cover the child's face with his hand.

Once an usher had seen Darnall grasp Bobby's jacket just as the child started to bolt when the villain seemed about to harm the heroine. But often, before they could stop him, Bobby would leap from his seat and dash into the aisle and out into the lobby.

The KiMo Theater was enormous, seating seven hundred. It was easy for a child to get lost and become panic stricken in its dark recesses. And then there was the story actors sometimes told of meeting the ghost of a pioneer woman walking through the darkened theater after rehearsals. Those who had seen her said she was attired in a calico dress and old-fashioned bonnet, but the manager simply pooh-poohed it. To the children, stories like that added a certain delicious eeriness to the theater.

Bobby loved westerns, and one day he saw a really old covered wagon for sale in front of a farm supply store. He began tugging on his father's arm, begging him to buy it.

"What on earth would we do with it?" asked his dad.

"It could be a playhouse for me," said Bobby. "I could spend the night out there."

Sometimes when Bobby stared over at the Sangre de Cristo Mountains, the past was so real to him it could all have been yesterday. "Why couldn't I have lived back then and been one of the early pioneers coming here?" he asked his dad.

"Because we can't choose when we want to live, Bobby. You might not want to have lived back then, because we don't know whether any of the people in this wagon reached here alive," said his dad running his fingers thoughtfully across a dark reddish brown stain on the floor of the wagon. "Some of them could have been killed by Indians."

"I think they got here," said Bobby. "I bet the pioneers who traveled in this wagon were good fighters and could beat off Indians. Let's get it, Dad."

"Buy it! Where would we put an old covered wagon, Bobby?"

"We could put it in our front yard."

"In our front yard!" exclaimed his father.

"Yes. I could use it for a playhouse. There's no tree for me to have a tree house like you had when you were a boy back east."

"That's true," said his father, and he gave in as he often did and bought it. Bobby and his friends played cowboys and Indians in it. Sometimes he and other boys in he neighborhood didn't even want to come in when it began to get dark.

"Can my friend Jerry and I spend the night out there?" he asked his mother.

"I don't think that's such a good idea," she said.

"What's the harm in it? Let him do it," protested his father. "I used to spend the night with some kids in the neighborhood in my tree house." And so they did, spending many a night in the old wagon.

Bobby dreamed he was the child of a family of pioneers and that they were headed west to Albuquerque.

"They were nice folks. I liked the mom in my dream," he told his mother when she asked him about it.

"Did the mom in your dream look like me?"

"How did you know?" he said, and he hugged her hard. "But you had on a long dress, and your clothes covered you up more."

"Well, that wouldn't hurt some of the women on the streets of Albuquerque today," commented his mother.

"Mom, why didn't I live back in exciting times like that?"

"You wouldn't have liked it as well as you think, Bobby. They didn't have movies or—" She stopped.

Bobby was already gone. He had shot out of the room, and she heard the back door opening. A wet, exuberant dog half ran, half slid across the kitchen toward her, stood on his hind legs, and put his front paws on her clean apron.

"Bobby! Bobby! Come get your dog right now!" she wailed in frustration. "You are going to have to teach this dog to behave—or he will have to stay outdoors!"

Bobby reappeared and grasped Zorro's collar.

"I will! I will! Don't worry, Mom. He's just a young dog and that's why he races from one place to another."

"You're the same way. You both need to stop dashing through the house this way. He's going to run across that street out there someday. Keep him inside the fence your dad fixed for him. He's got a doghouse out there to go into when it rains."

"But he likes to be indoors when it rains, Mom."

"Oh, all right! Get a towel and dry the both of you off."

Bobby bent down with a towel and began to dry Zorro and wipe his own tracks off the floor.

A few weeks later he came back from school and asked his mother for permission to go to the movies that Saturday afternoon with some of his friends.

"No, not without your father and me," said his mother. "You know how dark it is in the KiMo. Sometimes you get scared."

His father spoke up saying, "Your mother is right. And I hear there is a ghost in there." He thought that might discourage his son.

"What kind of ghost?"

"They say it's the ghost of a woman from pioneer days when Albuquerque was first settled."

"Oh, Dad, none of the kids ever said anything about that. Can't I go? They're not going at night—only in the afternoon," Bobby pleaded.

"I'm afraid you won't stay with them."

"Yes, I will, Mom."

"Let him go. He will be all right," said his father.

And Bobby went for the first time without his parents.

He sat with his friends, feeling as if he were a grown-up. He laughed a great deal during the first part of the film, which he thought was funny. Then it became exciting, and finally there was the villain's pursuit of the heroine. Bobby's heart began to beat faster, and he felt as if it would burst. He was sure the villain in the movie was going to hurt the girl—and then come after him! There was no father to seize his jacket and hold him. He jumped out of his seat, and heads turned as he pushed past the patrons in their seats in his row. Panic stricken he dashed along the aisle. "Stop!" cried an usher, but it was no use. Bobby had already reached the stairs and was hurrying down them. He headed toward the lobby.

Suddenly Bobby knew something terrible was happening. He felt the lobby floor shudder beneath his feet, and then there was an enormous boom. It was the last sound he would ever hear in this world. Gigantic pieces of the lobby floor blew into the air all around him. People on the floor above shrieked with terror, and everyone began running toward the exits. It was a long time later before men found Bobby's broken little body amidst the rubble of the lobby.

The spirit of the boy is said to have haunted the KiMo Theater for many years. The shadowy figure of a child has been seen running down the stairs or in the dark recesses of the floor below. But recently a visitor from another city to the remodeled theater told another story.

"I saw the ghost of a woman downstairs below the stage. She was wearing a long blue calico dress and a blue pioneer bonnet to match. She held a little boy by the hand. He was smiling with delight and so was she.

They were singing—the little boy's voice high and sweet and blending with the warm contralto of the woman—"Amazing grace, how sweet the sound, that saved . . ." The surprised visitor had edged closer to hear. The words of the music grew faint as the child and the pioneer woman walked into one of the dark and shadowy recesses beneath the theater, and then they were gone.

TOMBSTONE, ARIZONA, AND ITS NOTORIOUS GUNFIGHTERS

Tombstone. . . . Tombstone, Arizona. A place that stirs the imagination. In the shadow of the desolate Dragoon Mountains, stronghold of Cochise, and home for a time of one of the West's most famous lawmen, Wyatt Earp. Tombstone has all the magic of the past—the Crystal Palace where Wyatt Earp had his office on the second floor and ran a faro game downstairs, the Bird Cage Theater, the Lucky Cuss Bar, and the O.K. Corral.

Here in the 1880s came wealthy gamblers and some of the most notorious gunfighters of the West. Even today the town seems full of the shadowy figures of its violent past. Bat Masterson, Luke Short, Doc Holliday, and the Clanton brothers all walked these wooden sidewalks and rode the muddy streets of this town "too tough to die."

When a bearded prospector named Ed Schieffelin began to roam the lonely San Pedro Hills in search of silver, the soldiers at Fort Huachuca warned him of the dangerous Apaches, saying, "All you'll find here is your tombstone."

Schieffelin struck a rich silver vein in September of 1877 and boldly named it "The Tombstone." News of the rich strike brought the best and the worst of men hurrying to the town named after the strike that spawned it.

Two men arrived who were to make Tombstone even more famous. They were Wyatt Earp, who was to serve as deputy U.S. marshal, and John Clum, a courageous crusader of a man who began the newspaper— *The Tombstone Epitaph*. Both men were dedicated to wiping out crime, and they became good friends. In the pages of his paper, Clum strongly attacked the drunken cowboys who were terrorizing the town—calling them murderers and outlaws. Among them were Johnny Ringo, Buckskin Frank Leslie, Curly Bill Brocius—men who robbed and plundered helpless citizens throughout the Territory of Arizona. Clum became mayor and, despite threats on his life, used both the authority of his office and the influence of his paper to try to rid the town of lawlessness and terror.

War between the cowboys and the lawmen was soon to come. The McLaurys and the Clantons, who

were among the worst of the outlaws, had been taunting Wyatt Earp and his lawmen brothers, Virgil and Morgan, for weeks. Trouble began on the night of October 25, 1881, when a drunk and threatening Ike Clanton was arrested by Virgil Earp on a charge of disorderly conduct.

After jailing Clanton, Wyatt Earp went to the newspaper office to talk with his friend John Clum.

"They're all in town tonight, going from place to place, shooting off their gun, and making trouble," Earp told Clum. "I've sent word to Doc Holliday to come into town. We may need him."

When Holliday arrived, Wyatt Earp deputized him. There was no doubt that the lawmen were angry as the cowboys made their usual rounds of the gambling halls and saloons—rowdy and insulting wherever they went.

The next morning the Earps released Ike Clanton, hoping he and his friends would leave peacefully. As the cowboys mounted their horses at the O.K. Corral, the Earps and Doc Holliday watched and waited. The cowboys were boastful and appeared to be just spoiling for a fight. All were armed, and somebody fired a shot when the lawmen ordered the Clanton and McLaury brothers to drop their guns.

Advancing two or three steps from the crowd, Ike Clanton met Wyatt Earp's six-shooter.

"Throw up your hands," ordered Earp.

At the same time Tom McLaury made a move to draw his gun, and Bill Clanton reached for his. But Doc Holliday and Morgan Earp were quicker, and Bill Clanton dropped dead. Ike Clanton ran, managing to hide in the photo gallery, where he stayed while the guns barked outside.

When it was over, three men lay dead. Frank and Tom McLaury and Billy Clanton had been killed. The three Earp brothers and Doc Holliday were all wounded. It was Tombstone's bloodiest day.

John Clum worked far into the night gathering the details of the gun battle as he talked to the survivors and then began the tedious task of setting the letters of type by hand. Reaching into the case of large wood type, he picked out the letters for the headline— YESTERDAY'S TRAGEDY. Then he pulled out another drawer with smaller type—THREE MEN ARE HURLED INTO ETERNITY IN THE DURATION OF A MOMENT was the subhead. Then, letter by letter, the small type of the story was carefully put in place, and when he had finished, he carried the page over to the Washington hand press. The sun was rising as he finished printing his edition for the next day, but perhaps, at last, quieter times would be coming to Tombstone.

Clum continued the crusade in his paper against the cowboys and outlaws until the president of the United States threatened to send in soldiers and put the Arizona Territory under martial law. But the lawless element managed to buy out the interest of Clum's two partners, and when he lost control of the policy of the paper, he finally sold his own share and left Tombstone. His wife had died there, and he did not return until fifty years later when he came back to visit her grave.

Shortly after Clum left Tombstone, the mines began to fill with water, and soon most of them had water pumps operating twenty-four hours a day, but the pumps did not work well and more and more water seeped into the mines. When the country went back on the gold standard in the early 1890s, the price of silver dropped and the age of copper arrived. Miners left Tombstone and headed for the copper boomtowns. Many businesses closed, but *The Tombstone Epitaph* continued to be published and became known far and wide. It is still popular today. The name of John Clum was left on the front window and through it can be seen the old Washington hand press.

Recently a visitor to Tombstone named Tom Sherrill was unable to sleep. Leaving his motel room, he walked through the quiet village. He paused beside the big tree in front of *The Tombstone Epitaph*, then decided that he heard a noise and went over to stare in the window. It was the sound of a printing press—kaplam, kaplam, kaplam, over and over. It was a strange sound out of the distant past, and as he listened, he saw the figure of a man bending over the Washington press, working away.

He watched in amazement, and finally the sound stopped. The spectral figure gathered a large bundle of papers, opened the door of the *Epitaph*, and began walking toward Allen Street. Sherrill decided to follow. At the corner the door of the Crystal Palace swung open, and a man who must have been a cowboy reached for a paper and then disappeared. Whoever was carrying the papers, man or phantom, turned—almost colliding with Sherrill, much to his fright—but without appearing to see him, walked across the street to the Oriental Saloon on the other corner. Again the doors opened, and this time it seemed to Sherrill to be a woman who reached out her arms for some papers.

Now he saw a form on horseback about a block down Allen Street riding toward him. But instead the horse and rider stopped at the Wells Fargo office. The apparition crossed the street and handed a paper to the rider of the horse and then bent down as if tying up a packet of the papers to leave at the doorway of the Wells Fargo office. He continued on his way with Sherrill not far behind.

The phantasmic figure carrying its papers turned right on Toughnut Street, passed the miner's cabins, throwing out one paper here and one there, left a few at the door of the law offices often referred to as "Rotten Row," and headed toward the courthouse. The gallows were located at the side. Watching him leave several papers at the door of the courthouse, Sherrill decided to go up the steps and pick up one of the copies. He reached down and passed his fingers along the doorsill, closing his hand on something, but when he opened it, all he had was a fistful of cobwebs. They were not only sticky, but they were wet and shiny and black. He could have taken them to a chemist to be analyzed, but Robert Sherrill was an old-time newspaper man, and he did not have to take printer's ink to a chemist to be told what it was!

Sometimes a person longs to return to a moment in time when their whole life converged in a single place. For a prospector it may be the moment he makes his richest strike. For a newspaper editor in Tombstone, Arizona, perhaps it is the moment he realizes he is going to press with the biggest story of his life. The most famous gunfight of the West—the gunfight at the O.K. Corral—has happened at his very door.

And so on an October night the old press clatters away, and a man long dead returns from another world to go out to deliver his phantom papers.

THE ENCHANTED ROCK

Turning off on Highway 965 at Llano, Texas, was not a sudden decision for Terry Blackwelder. It was the road that led to a place that had always fascinated him—the Enchanted Rock. His interest in the rock and the dramatic batholith formations there began during an anthropology course in college when he learned that he probably had Indian blood in his veins.

When he was a little boy, his grandfather would look at him and say, "See these high cheekbones and coal black hair? There is an Indian in this boy's background somewhere."

But many tribes had traveled through this area that would someday become Texas and had visited the Enchanted Rock. Which tribe was it? This was the domain of the Lipan Apaches and Tonkawas. The Tonkawas

lived by hunting, gathering, and fishing. Later they were taken over by the dangerous and feared Wichitas and the Comanches, whose major occupation was the warpath!

Terry knew that this was a place the plains Indians regarded with awe and fear. It was here they experienced the supernatural. Here spirits and demons appeared and were worshipped by the Indian people. The braves danced elaborate dances and held ceremonies in an effort to pacify and control the spirits. Terry knew this as a student knows it, but it did not hold the same awe or sense of excitement for him as it had for the people of these early tribes.

He watched a hawk glide and circle down effortlessly, avoiding a soaptree yucca plant, until it landed not far from the base of one of the great rocks. Around it was a sea of blue flowers. He was conscious of the fragrance of bee brush, agarito, and persimmon that suffused the air.

At the foot of the rock the sagebrush with its coarsetoothed near-white leaves grew outward from the base of the mountains toward the harsh dry plains. He recognized the fragrant scent of its branches, which some Indians still burned as a ceremonial incense.

Humans had visited this dramatic rock formation for more than eleven thousand years—not only because it was on a trading route that led south toward other Indian tribes but also because they believed in the supernatural qualities of the rock itself. Trips were made here at times of extreme tribal need. They came to consult the spirits of the Enchanted Rock before making war or in the event of a prolonged drought.

Now the massive pinkish domes of stone came into view ahead of Terry. The rock's enormous dome, towering more than four hundred feet high, dominated the area. Terry, carrying his camping gear, began to make his way up the steep summit trail on the western side to the rock's crest. Ahead the sun became a smoldering red backdrop as it began to slide below the horizon. It should be a beautiful view tonight Terry thought. He did not notice until he left the trail briefly and looked back that all the visitors' cars had left.

As he gazed down, a necklace of bonfires began to spring up below him. To his amazement he saw a throng of sweat-slick, brightly painted people gyrating and leading the others in a wild dance around the base of the mountainous rock. Some of them seemed to be in the lead, urging a procession of children with flowers in their hair up the steep trail. Now they had reached the top of the rock. It was eerie, for despite the frenzied activity, Terry heard no sound. Male figures led the rites, writhing and gesticulating, urging the others on.

He redoubled his efforts to reach the crest. There were tiny sparks that he thought must be emerging stars in the rapidly falling darkness above his head, but he soon realized they were not stars. Were these the "ghost fires" said to flicker all around the top?

He had once heard that a Spanish conquistador captured by the Tonkawas had escaped a terrible death and lost himself in the area. Fortunately for him the Indians never found him, but they believed that his spirit stayed and wove enchantments against them on top of the rock.

Then he heard a truly frightening sound—a weird creaking and groaning. It was eerie and seemed to rise from all around him. Were they the protests of some ancient Indian gods?

He removed a blanket from his gear, unfolded it, and, sitting there, stared into the bonfires. Turning back to watch the knot of people gathered across from him on the edge of the crest, he looked on in horror as the figure of the little girl swayed, tottered, and then, with a piercing shriek, began to fall.

Now he began to recall some of the darker stories of Indian rituals of the past and of human sacrifice. He began to feel sick. Saying under his breath, "Help me, Jesus!" he blacked out.

When he awoke, stiff and sore, the sun was rising in the east. But he could not rid his mind of the wildly gyrating figures of the night before as he drove home. Had they only been a dream? Gradually they began to fade—as did his interest in his Indian ancestry.

A speaker at the college several months later brought some of the horror back. "Cannibalism and human sacrifice were rare," he said with a deprecating smile. "And the spirits said to be up there are only figments of our imagination." But Terry was not so sure. The Tonkawa Indians believed ghost fires flickered atop the Enchanted Rock, and they had also heard weird creaking and groaning.

Although geologists today say this is only the rock expanding in the heat of the day and then contracting in the cool of the evening, to listen to it up there at night is still an awesome thing.

This huge, pink granite dome of a rock that rises 1,825 feet above sea level and covers 640 acres is one of the largest batholiths—underlying rock formations uncovered by erosion—in the United States. It was designated a National Natural Landmark in 1984 and is known as the Enchanted Rock State Natural Area. The park is north of Fredericksburg, Texas, on the border between Gillespie and Llano counties.